Animaths

Multiples

with Meerkats

Tracey Steffora

Raintree is an imprint of Capstone Global Library Limited, a company incorporated in England and Wales having its registered office at 7 Pilgrim Street, London, EC4V 6LB – Registered company number: 6695582

To contact Raintree:
Phone: 0845 6044371
Fax: + 44 (0) 1865 312263
Email: myorders@raintreepublishers.co.uk
Outside the UK please telephone
+44 1865 312262.

Edited by Daniel Nunn, Abby Colich and Sian Smith
Designed by Joanna Hinton-Malivoire
Picture research by Elizabeth Alexander
Production by Victoria Fitzgerald
Originated by Capstone Global Library Ltd
Printed and bound in China by Leo Paper Products Ltd

ISBN 978 1 4062 6052 6
17 16 15 14 13
10 9 8 7 6 5 4 3 2 1

British Library Cataloguing in Publication Data
A full catalogue record for this book is available from the British Library.

Acknowledgements
We would like to thank the following for permission to reproduce photographs: Dreamtime.com p.12 (© Fotomicar); Shutterstock pp.4 (© AnetaPics), 5 (© tratong), 6, 7, 8, 9, 11, 16, 17, 19, 21 (© Eric Isselee), 10 (© Karol Kozlowski), 13, 14, 15 (© arka38).

Front and back cover photographs of meerkats reproduced with permission of Shutterstock (© Eric Isselée).

We would like to thank Elaine Bennett for her invaluable help in the preparation of this book.

Every effort has been made to contact copyright holders of material reproduced in this book. Any omissions will be rectified in subsequent printings if notice is given to the publisher.

Contents

Some words are shown in bold, **like this**. You can find them in a glossary on page 23.

Multiples with meerkats

Meerkats live in deserts in Africa. They live in large groups called **mobs**.

When there are many things to count, we can put them into groups to make the counting go faster. Let's count a mob of meerkats!

Counting in 2s

Start with two meerkat **pups**.

Add two more.

$$2 + 2 = 4$$

Two plus two is four. There are **double** the meerkat pups.

Here are two more meerkat pups!
Let's add them on.

There are two meerkats in each group.
There are three groups of two. Add the
groups together.

2 + 2 + 2 = 6

There are six meerkats in all.

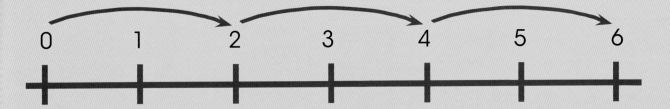

When we add the same numbers together, we can also use **multiples** to find the answer.

How many meerkats are in this **mob**?

Count in **multiples** of two to find out!

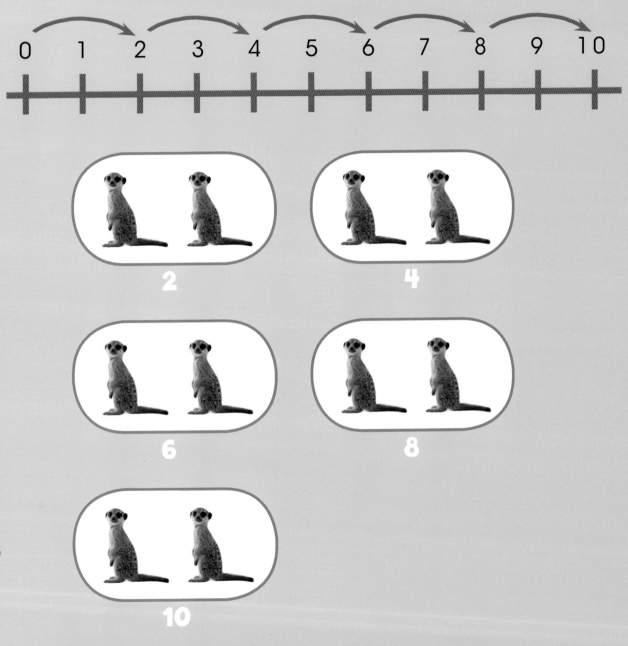

0 1 2 3 4 5 6 7 8 9 10

2

4

6

8

10

There are ten meerkats in the mob.

Meerkats get hungry! This meerkat is eating a scorpion.

Look at all these scorpions! Let's use **multiples** to find out how many there are.

We can count in **multiples** of two.

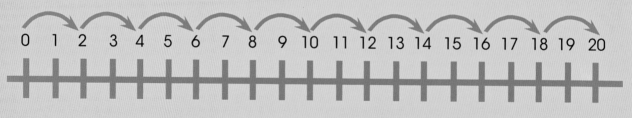

 2

 4

6

 8

 10

12

 14

16

18

 20

There are twenty scorpions in all.

Counting in 5s

We can also count in multiples of five!

0 1 2 3 4 5 6 7 8 9 10 11 12 13 14 15 16 17 18 19 20

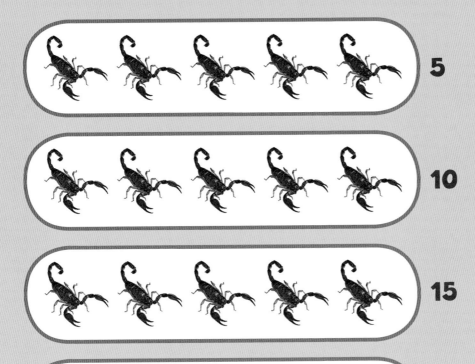

5

10

15

20

There are plenty of scorpions for lunch!

There can be a lot of meerkats in one **mob**. Look at all these meerkats! It would take a long time to count each one. Counting in **multiples** is faster!

Put the meerkats in groups of five. Count in 5s to find out how many there are altogether.

5 10 15 20 25

30 35 40 45 50

There are fifty meerkats in all!

Counting in 10s

We can also count in **multiples** of ten. Look at the pattern. All the numbers end in zero.

10 ten

20 twenty

30 thirty

40 forty

50 fifty

60 sixty

70 seventy

80 eighty

90 ninety

100 one hundred

Now put the meerkats in groups of ten and use multiples to count to fifty.

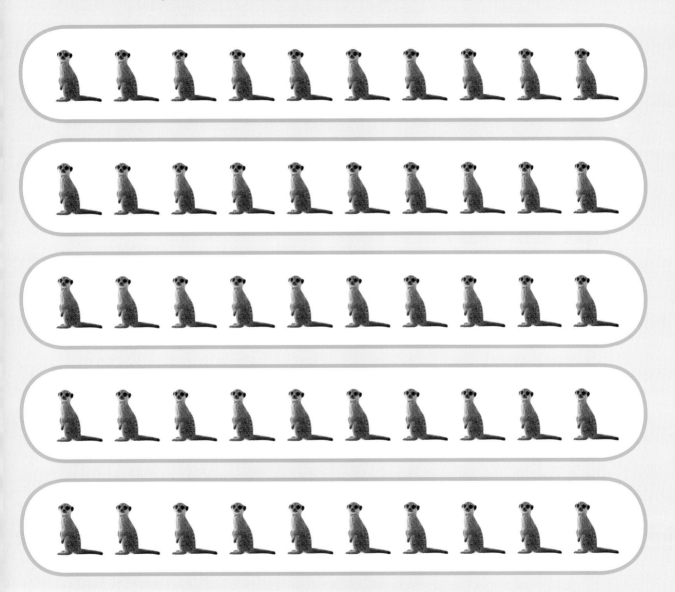

Using multiples of ten is even faster than using multiples of five!

19

Hundred chart

This hundred chart shows numbers in a pattern. It can help you to count using **multiples** of five and ten.

1	2	3	4	5	6	7	8	9	10
11	12	13	14	15	16	17	18	19	20
21	22	23	24	25	26	27	28	29	30
31	32	33	34	35	36	37	38	39	40
41	42	43	44	45	46	47	48	49	50
51	52	53	54	55	56	57	58	59	60
61	62	63	64	65	66	67	68	69	70
71	72	73	74	75	76	77	78	79	80
81	82	83	84	85	86	87	88	89	90
91	92	93	94	95	96	97	98	99	100

Look! There are many meerkats!

How many are there? Count in multiples of ten to find out.

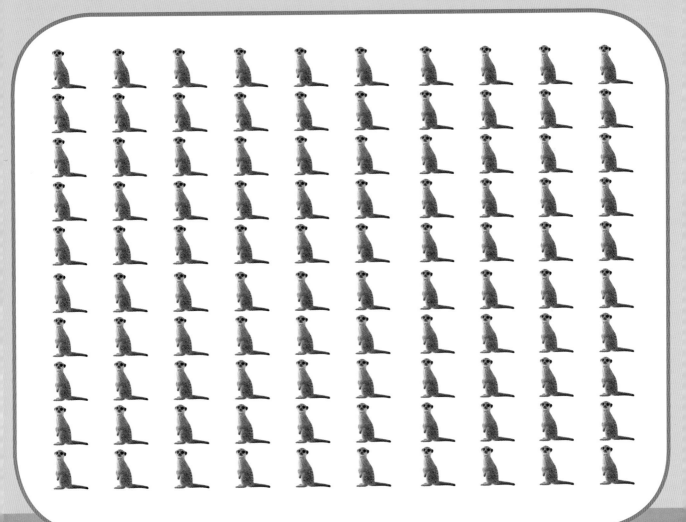

Answer on page 22.

21

Meerkat facts

- Meerkats often live in groups of about 20, but there can be 50 or more meerkats in a **mob**.

- Meerkats stand up tall to look out for danger. One member of the group is always watching out for enemies.

- Meerkats are not cats. They are members of the mongoose family.

- Meerkats mostly eat insects, but they also eat scorpions, lizards, and plants.

Maths glossary

double to have twice as much of something

multiples groups of numbers that go up by the same amount each time

For example:

    2, 4, 6, 8, and 10 are multiples of 2

    5, 10, 15, 20, and 25 are multiples of 5

    10, 20, 30, 40, and 50 are multiples of 10

Meerkat glossary

mob a group of meerkats

pup a young meerkat

Index